The Best 50
DESSERT TARTS

Sandra Rudloff

BRISTOL PUBLISHING ENTERPRISES
Hayward, California

Printed in the United States of America.

ISBN: 1-55867-283-4

Cover design: Frank J. Paredes
Cover photography: John A. Benson
Food stylist: Susan Devaty
Illustration: Caryn Leschen

PIES AND TARTS:
WHAT'S THE DIFFERENCE?

What is the difference between a pie and a tart? Both are baked in crusts and can have a variety of fillings. The fillings can be cooked on the stovetop and poured into a baked crust, or filling and crust can be baked together in the oven. So, they're very similar.

Tarts, however, are cooked in a flat-bottomed tart pan with removable sides (similar to a spring form pan). When serving a tart, the sides of the pan are removed, making a freestanding dessert. Because of this, tarts are about half the thickness of most pies.

All the recipes in this book have been created using a 9-inch tart pan. You can use a different-sized pan by adjusting the ingredient quantities as follows:

- For a 7-inch tart pan use ½ the ingredients
- For an 8-inch tart pan use the same ingredients

- For a 7-x-10-inch rectangular tart pan use the same ingredients
- For a 12-inch tart pan use 1⅓ times the ingredients

CRUSTS

Following are three tart crusts. You can also use any favorite pie crust recipe you may have. If you are short on time, you can use any prepared pie crust you choose — just fit it to your tart pan.

SWEET COOKIE CRUST

This crust is similar in texture to shortbread.

1 1/2 cups all-purpose flour
1/3 cup granulated sugar
1/4 tsp. salt

1/2 cup shortening
2 tbs. milk
2 egg yolks

In a medium bowl, stir together flour, sugar and salt until mixed. Cut shortening into flour mixture until mixture resembles a fine crumb.

In a small bowl, mix together milk and egg yolks until smooth. Stir into flour mixture to moisten. The mixture should remain crumbly and not form into a paste.

Sprinkle mixture into a tart pan. Pat into the pan bottom and up the sides, keeping the thickness even throughout.

Bake for 15 minutes at 400° if using as a pre-baked crust.

PASTRY NUT CRUST

The best nuts to use in this crust are walnuts, peanuts, almonds and macadamias. Use care if using other nuts, as the oil content may cause excessive browning.

1 cup all-purpose flour
$1/2$ cup butter
$1/4$ cup granulated sugar
$1/3$ cup finely chopped nuts

Mix all ingredients together in a medium bowl. Press into the bottom and up the sides of a tart pan.

Bake for 10 to 12 minutes at 400° if using as a pre-baked crust.

RICH PASTRY CRUST

This rolled crust will give you a crust similar to piecrust.

1½ cups all-purpose flour
1 tbs. granulated sugar
¼ tsp. salt

⅓ cup shortening or butter
3 tbs. ice-cold water

Mix flour, sugar and salt together in a medium bowl. Cut shortening or butter into flour until mixture resembles a fine crumb. Sprinkle in cold water 1 tbs. at a time; mix gently after each addition. Add water just until pastry holds together. Shape into a ball, wrap in plastic wrap and refrigerate for 2 hours.

Lightly flour a work surface. Place dough onto surface and roll dough out to a 10- to 11-inch circle. Press into a tart pan and shape around edges as needed.

Bake for 10 to 12 minutes at 400° (until lightly golden) if using as a pre-baked crust.

APPLE, PEAR, AND DRIED CHERRY TART

The combination of fruits is a nice way to say goodbye to summer and hello to autumn. Tart cherries will give the best flavor.

¼ cup Kirsch or Calvados liqueur
1 cup finely chopped dried cherries
3 Bosc or Anjou pears
3 Granny Smith apples
2 tbs. fresh lemon juice
½ cup granulated sugar
1½ tbs. cornstarch
1 unbaked tart crust

Heat oven to 400°. In a small saucepan, bring liqueur to a boil. Add cherries and stir to mix. Remove from heat, cover and set aside for 30 minutes.

Peel and core pears and apples. Cut into medium chunks. Place into a large bowl and add lemon juice. Toss to coat. In a small bowl, combine sugar and cornstarch. Add cherries and any remaining liquid to apples and pears. Toss to mix. Sprinkle sugar mixture over fruit and toss to mix.

Pour fruit into prepared tart crust. Bake for 50 to 60 minutes, or until pears and apples are tender and crust is golden. Remove from oven and let cool on rack. Serve warm or refrigerate until chilled.

CARDAMOM APPLE TART

Cardamom is a spice similar in taste to ginger or cloves. It is used frequently in Scandinavian cooking. This is especially good served warm with lightly sweetened whipped cream.

4 large Granny Smith apples
1/2 cup granulated sugar
1/2 tsp. ground cardamom
1 unbaked tart crust (*Rich Pastry Crust,* page 5, suggested)
2 tbs. butter, cut into 1/2-inch pieces

Heat oven to 400°. Peel and core apples and slice into 1/4-inch-thick slices. Place apples in a medium bowl and sprinkle sugar and cardamom over them. Toss to coat evenly.

Place apple mixture in prepared tart crust. Dot apples with butter pieces. Bake for 40 to 45 minutes, or until crust is golden.

HONEY APPLE TART

Just a few ingredients go into this tart, which should be served warm. This is a favorite to make when the days are cold.

4 large Granny Smith apples
2 tbs. butter
1/2 cup honey
1 unbaked tart crust

Heat oven to 400°. Peel and core apples and slice into 1/4-inch-thick slices. Heat butter in a large skillet over medium heat. Add apples and sauté until tender and apples are dry, about 15 minutes. Remove from heat. Add honey and toss until coated.

Place apple mixture into prepared tart crust. Bake for 25 to 35 minutes, or until crust is golden.

CRANBERRY APPLE TART

A cooked cranberry sauce is tossed with apples and everything baked together. This makes a change from traditional apple pies for the holidays.

2 cups fresh cranberries
1 cup apple juice
1½ cups granulated sugar, divided
4 Granny Smith apples
⅓ cup flour
1 tsp. cinnamon
1 unbaked tart crust

Heat oven to 425°. In a small saucepan, combine cranberries, apple juice and 1 cup of the sugar. Bring to a boil over medium heat, stirring occasionally. Reduce heat to low and cook for 25 minutes. You should have about 1½ cups of cranberry sauce. Remove from heat and cool.

Peel and core apples and cut into small chunks. Add cranberry mixture to apples and stir to mix. In a small bowl, mix together flour, cinnamon and remaining sugar. Add to cranberry apple mixture and stir to mix well.

Pour into prepared crust and bake for 45 to 50 minutes. Remove from oven and cool. Serve warm, or refrigerate until chilled.

TARTE TARTIN
(CLASSIC GLAZED APPLE TART)

This is the classic apple tart. The traditional way is to cook apples in a skillet, place dough on top and bake in the oven. This version has apples sautéed in butter, arranged in a crust and baked to finish. It is a bit work-intensive, but gives a beautiful display of apples under a shiny glaze. This is best served shortly after baking or at room temperature.

6 Granny Smith apples
1/4 cup butter
1/4 cup granulated sugar
1 tsp. lemon juice
1/2 cup apple or apricot jelly
1 unbaked tart crust

Heat oven to 400°. Peel and core apples and cut into ¼-inch-thick slices. Melt butter over medium heat in a large, nonstick skillet. Add apples and sauté until just tender, about 15 minutes. Sprinkle in sugar and lemon juice and stir to mix.

Place apple slices in prepared crust, overlapping slices in a circular pattern. Continue this process in layers until all apples have been placed.

Bake for 30 to 40 minutes or until crust is browned and apples are tender. Remove from oven.

Heat jelly in a small pan until boiling. Brush evenly over cooked tart. Serve warm or at room temperature.

GINGER PEAR TART

Pears and ginger are a favorite taste pairing. Be sure to use only Anjou or Bosc pears, as they are firmer and have less juice than other varieties.

1½ tsp. ground ginger
2 tbs. cornstarch
⅔ cup granulated sugar
6 large Anjou or Bosc pears
1 unbaked tart crust

Heat oven to 425°. In a large bowl, combine ginger, cornstarch and sugar and mix well.

Peel, quarter and core pears. Cut into large chunks and add to ginger mixture. Toss gently to coat pears evenly.

Place in prepared crust and bake for 45 to 55 minutes. Remove from oven and let cool. Serve lukewarm or at room temperature.

SWEET PEACH TART

Fresh peaches and brown sugar make a summer sweet treat. Topped with vanilla ice cream, this becomes heavenly.

1/2 cup brown sugar, packed
2 tbs. cornstarch
1/4 tsp. cinnamon
6 large peaches

1 tbs. freshly squeezed lemon
   juice
1 unbaked tart crust

Heat oven to 425°. In a large bowl, mix together brown sugar, cornstarch and cinnamon and set aside. Peel and pit peaches. Thickly slice peaches (1/2 inch to 1 inch thick). Work quickly so peaches do not discolor. As you slice a peach, sprinkle a bit of the lemon juice over it, and toss peaches to help keep from browning. Sprinkle brown sugar mixture over peaches and toss gently to mix.

Pour mixture into prepared crust and bake for 40 to 50 minutes. Serve warm, or refrigerate and serve chilled.

ITALIAN PLUM TART

You can use red or black plums, whichever you prefer. You can even use yellow plums, but the color of the red or black plums is far prettier. Regular granulated sugar can be substituted for raw sugar.

$1/2$ cup raw sugar
$1 1/2$ tbs. cornstarch
$1 1/2$ fresh ripe plums, halved and pitted
1 tbs. apple juice
1 unbaked tart crust (*Sweet Cookie Crust,* page 3, suggested)

Heat oven to 400°. In a large bowl, combine sugar and cornstarch. Add plums and apple juice and toss to coat. Let stand, stirring occasionally, for 30 minutes, or until the plums have released some of their juices, and sugar has dissolved.

Arrange plums skin-side down in prepared tart crust. Slice any remaining plum halves into thick slices and tuck between halves in crust. Pour juices over plums. Cover tart loosely with foil.

Bake for 30 minutes. Remove foil and bake for an additional 20 to 30 minutes, or until plums are tender and crust is lightly browned. Remove from oven and cool on rack. Serve at room temperature.

APRICOT TART

Our apricot tree gives a huge amount of sweet, honey-flavored apricots every summer. They're perfect for jams, tarts and pastries. Make this tart with macadamia- or almond-flavored Pastry Nut Crust, *page 4.*

$1/2$ cup sour cream	1 tbs. flour
1 egg, beaten	1 unbaked tart crust
3 tbs. honey, divided	$1 1/2$ lb. fresh apricots

Heat oven to 375°. In a medium bowl, mix together sour cream, egg and 2 tbs. of the honey. Sprinkle in flour and beat until well mixed. Pour into prepared tart crust. Halve and pit apricots and place skin-side down over filling. Slice up any remaining halves and tuck into spaces on tart.

Bake for 50 to 60 minutes. Remove from oven. Heat remaining honey in a small saucepan or microwave-safe dish until warm and thinned. Brush honey over apricots. Serve at room temperature, or slightly warm.

SHAKER LEMON TART

This tart is a variation on Shaker Lemon Pie, which used fresh slices of lemon, rind and all, in a single crust. I find the texture of the baked rinds too chewy, so this version uses peeled lemons.

3 large lemons, peeled
2 cups granulated sugar

4 eggs, beaten
1 unbaked tart crust

Heat oven to 400°. Slice lemons paper-thin. Sprinkle 1/2 cup of the sugar into the bottom of a glass or plastic bowl. Place 1/3 of the sliced lemons on top of sugar. Continue to layer sugar and lemons, ending with sugar. Let stand at room temperature for 2 to 4 hours. Remove lemon slices from sugar and set aside. Add eggs to sugar and juice in bowl and mix well. Return slices to bowl and gently mix, taking care not to break up slices. Gently place lemon slices into prepared crust. Pour any remaining egg mixture over the top. Bake for 30 to 45 minutes, or until a knife inserted in the middle of filling comes out clean. Remove from oven and let cool to room temperature.

BLACKBERRY SPICE TART

This tart can be made anytime of year, thanks to the availability of frozen blackberries.

4 cups fresh or frozen
   blackberries*
1/2 cup granulated sugar
3 tbs. all-purpose flour

1/2 tsp. ground cinnamon
1/2 tsp. ground nutmeg
1/2 tsp. ground allspice
1 unbaked tart crust

* Note: if using frozen blackberries, measure berries when they are frozen, but be sure to allow berries to completely defrost prior to assembling the tart.

Heat oven to 425°. In a large bowl, combine berries, sugar, flour, cinnamon, nutmeg and allspice. Toss together until well mixed. Place berry mixture into prepared tart crust.

Bake for about 45 minutes. Remove from oven and let cool slightly before serving; or allow to cool completely and serve chilled.

BLUEBERRY BUTTERMILK TART

Creamy and sweet, this must be made with fresh blueberries; frozen and canned berries have too much liquid.

1 cup buttermilk
1/4 cup melted butter
3 large egg yolks
1/2 cup granulated sugar
1 tsp. vanilla extract

1 tbs. grated lemon rind
1 tbs. fresh lemon juice
1 tbs. flour
2 cups fresh blueberries
1 unbaked tart crust

Heat oven to 350°. In a blender, combine buttermilk, butter, egg yolks, sugar, vanilla, rind, juice and flour. Pulse until smooth. Spread blueberries in prepared tart crust and pour batter over them, filling pie shell near to the top.

Bake for 1 hour or until batter is set. (When you touch it slightly, your finger should bounce off, not sink.) Cool for at least 1 hour and serve at room temperature.

MIXED BERRY TART

This tart uses summer berries and a hint of lemon for its filling. Frozen berries can also be used — just defrost and bring them to room temperature before beginning.

1 cup strawberries, halved
1 cup raspberries
1 cup blueberries
1 cup blackberries
1 tbs. freshly squeezed lemon juice

grated zest of 1 lemon
1 cup granulated sugar
¼ cup flour
1 tbs. tapioca
1 unbaked tart crust

Heat oven to 425°. In a large bowl, gently mix together berries, lemon juice and zest. In a small bowl, mix together sugar, flour and tapioca. Sprinkle flour mixture over berries and gently toss to coat. Try not to crush berries when mixing. Spoon mixture into prepared tart crust and bake for 35 to 45 minutes. Remove from oven. Serve warm or chilled.

LATE SUMMER BERRY TART

This uses the best of late summer berries, and adds a bit of rhubarb for tartness. You can make this any time of year, thanks to the availability of frozen berries.

1 cup diced fresh rhubarb
1½ cups blackberries
1½ cups raspberries

1¼ cups granulated sugar
¼ cup flour
1 unbaked tart crust

Heat oven to 350°. In a small bowl, mix together rhubarb, blackberries and raspberries. In another bowl, stir together sugar and flour. Add sugar mixture to berries and toss to coat. Pour berry mixture into prepared tart crust.

Bake for 45 to 55 minutes, or until crust is golden and berry mixture is bubbling. Remove from oven. Serve warm, or let cool and refrigerate until chilled.

CAFFE LATTE TART

This easy-to-make custard tart tastes like a sweet caffe latte. If you don't have an espresso machine, just use really strong coffee.

4 eggs
1/3 cup granulated sugar
1 1/2 cups milk

1 cup espresso, cooled
1/2 tsp. vanilla extract
1 unbaked tart crust

Heat oven to 450°. Beat eggs and sugar together until well mixed. Add milk, espresso and vanilla and stir to mix.

Pour into prepared tart crust and bake for 10 minutes. Reduce heat to 350° and bake until custard is set, about 30 minutes longer, or until a knife inserted in the center comes out clean.

WALNUT TART

If you like pecan pie, you'll enjoy this sweet and nutty tart, too. Served warm with whipped cream, it is a delicious dessert any time of year.

1 cup light brown sugar, packed
½ cup granulated sugar
1 tbs. all-purpose flour
2 eggs
2 tbs. heavy cream

1 tsp. vanilla extract
½ cup melted butter
1 cup chopped walnuts
1 unbaked tart crust (*Rich Pastry Crust*, page 5, suggested)

Heat oven to 375°. In a large bowl, mix together brown sugar, granulated sugar and flour until blended. Add eggs, cream, vanilla and butter and stir to mix. Fold in walnuts.

Pour mixture into prepared tart crust and bake for 35 to 45 minutes. Cool slightly and serve warm.

BEE STING TART

This tart has an almond paste base, with honey almonds and coconut on top. Serve with lightly sweetened whipped cream.

Filling

3/4 cup almonds
1/2 cup granulated sugar
1 tsp. vanilla extract
1/4 cup butter
2 eggs
1/4 all-purpose flour

1 unbaked tart crust

Topping

6 tbs. butter, softened
1/4 cup honey
1/4 cup granulated sugar
1/4 cup shredded coconut
3/4 cup sliced almonds

Heat oven to 350°. Combine almonds and sugar in a food processor workbowl or blender container. Pulse until finely ground (mixture should look like wet sand). Add vanilla and butter and pulse until completely mixed. Add eggs and pulse until smooth. Remove from workbowl and place in a medium bowl. Stir in flour by hand until well incorporated. Spread into prepared tart crust.

Combine butter, honey, sugar, coconut and sliced almonds together until mixed. Gently spread over almond filling.

Bake for 30 to 40 minutes, or until topping is caramelized and golden.

Cool on a rack to room temperature before serving.

MAPLE WALNUT TART

I remember an ice cream called "Black Walnut", which was just a maple ice cream studded with walnuts. Be sure to use real maple syrup, and not the maple-flavored pancake syrup commonly available.

1/2 cup granulated sugar
2 tbs. flour
3 eggs
1 cup maple syrup

1/4 cup butter, melted
1 cup chopped walnuts
1 unbaked tart crust

Heat oven to 375°. In a large bowl, mix together sugar and flour. Stir in eggs, maple syrup and melted butter. Fold in walnuts.

Pour mixture into prepared tart crust and bake for 35 to 45 minutes. Cool slightly and serve warm.

PINE NUT TART

Honey, studded with lots of pine nuts, flavors this caramel-type filling.

3/4 cup heavy cream
3/4 cup granulated sugar
1/3 cup honey
2 tbs. butter

1 1/2 cups pine nuts
1 pre-baked tart crust (*Sweet Cookie Crust*, page 3, or *Rich Pastry Crust*, page 5, suggested)

Heat oven to 375°. In a medium saucepan, mix together cream, sugar, honey and butter. Bring to a boil over medium heat, stirring constantly. Boil without stirring for 2 minutes. Remove from heat and stir in pine nuts. Refrigerate until filling is thick, about 45 minutes.

Pour filling into prepared tart crust and bake until filling is golden brown and bubbles, about 15 to 20 minutes. Remove from oven and let cool. Serve at room temperature.

CHOCOLATE TRUFFLE TART

This tart is very rich, and I like to make it using the Sweet Cookie Crust, *page 3. Serve with your favorite ice cream, or top with a caramel sauce.*

8 oz. semisweet chocolate chips
1/2 cup unsalted butter
2 tbs. instant coffee

2 tbs. light or dark rum
3 eggs
1 unbaked tart crust

Heat oven to 375°. In a medium saucepan, melt together chocolate and butter, stirring constantly until smooth. Remove from heat and stir in instant coffee and rum. Cool for 30 minutes.

Beat eggs in a small bowl until light and frothy. Fold into chocolate mixture. Pour into prepared tart crust. Bake for 25 to 30 minutes. Tart will be a bit soft in the center, but will continue to cook out of the oven. Cool for 2 hours on a rack and then place in refrigerator until firm, about 1 1/2 hours.

CHOCOLATE NUT TART

Although I love the pairing of chocolate and walnuts, others rave about chocolate and macadamia nuts or chocolate and almonds. Use your favorite and you will be in chocolate heaven.

$\frac{1}{2}$ cup butter
3 one-ounce squares
   unsweetened chocolate
$1\frac{1}{4}$ cups light brown sugar,
   packed
2 tbs. flour

2 eggs
1 tsp. vanilla extract
$1\frac{1}{2}$ cups chopped nuts (walnuts,
   almonds, macadamia, pecans,
   hazelnuts or other)
1 unbaked tart crust

Heat oven to 350°. In a small saucepan, melt together butter and chocolate. Stir in brown sugar and flour and mix until smooth. Add eggs, vanilla and nuts. Pour chocolate mixture into prepared tart crust.

Bake for 30 to 40 minutes, or until filling is set. Remove from oven and cool on rack. Refrigerate for at least 1 hour before serving.

CHOCOLATE CHUNK TART

Use high quality chocolate for this tart, as you'll want to savor the contrasting flavors in each bite.

4 eggs
1/2 cup granulated sugar
1 1/2 cups half-and-half
1 tsp. vanilla extract
4 oz. bittersweet chocolate, chopped into chunks

4 oz. milk chocolate, chopped into chunks
4 oz. white chocolate, chopped into chunks
1 pre-baked tart crust

Heat oven to 375°. In a large bowl, mix together eggs and sugar until light. Add half-and-half and vanilla and beat to mix well. Stir in chocolate chunks.

Pour mixture into prepared tart crust. Bake for 40 to 50 minutes, or until a knife inserted in the center comes out clean. Let cool on rack and then refrigerate until serving.

SWEET POTATO AND HONEY TART

Sweet potato pie is a rich dessert, and usually made with brown sugar or molasses. Honey makes a nice variation.

1 1/2 cups mashed sweet potatoes
2/3 cup honey
1 egg, beaten
1 cup milk
1 tsp. cinnamon
1/2 tsp. ground ginger

1/4 tsp. allspice
1 pinch salt
sugared walnut or pecan halves, optional
1 unbaked tart crust

Heat oven to 405°. Combine all ingredients in a large bowl, mixing until smooth. Pour into prepared tart crust. Bake in oven for 15 minutes.

Reduce heat to 350° and continue baking for 30 minutes, or until a knife inserted in the center comes out clean.

If desired, gently press sugared nuts into top of cooked tart after removing from oven.

PUMPKIN PECAN TART

Sweet and crunchy pecans top the creamy pumpkin filling in this tart. For an autumn treat, I make this using Sweet Cookie Crust, *page 3.*

Filling
1 cup half-and-half
2 eggs
1½ cups pumpkin
⅔ cup brown sugar, packed
1 tsp. ground cinnamon
½ tsp. ground ginger
½ tsp. ground cloves
½ tsp. allspice
1 tsp. vanilla extract

1 unbaked tart crust

Topping
1 cup chopped pecans
1 tsp. ground cinnamon
½ cup brown sugar, packed
2 tbs. butter, melted

Heat oven to 400°. Combine all filling ingredients in a large bowl. Using an electric mixer, mix on medium until well blended. Pour into prepared tart crust. Bake for 35 to 45 minutes. Remove from oven and let cool on rack.

To prepare topping, mix together nuts, cinnamon and brown sugar. Stir in butter until moistened.

Sprinkle topping over pumpkin filling. Place under a hot broiler for 1 to 2 minutes, taking care not to burn crust or nuts. Serve immediately.

RUM RAISIN TART

This is a very old fashioned dessert, but one that everyone loves. A giant scoop of vanilla ice cream is delicious on top.

2 cups raisins
1/2 cup apple juice
1/4 cup rum
1/2–3/4 cup granulated sugar

2 tbs. flour
1/4 tsp. salt
1 unbaked tart crust

Heat oven to 450°. In a medium saucepan, combine raisins, apple juice and rum. Bring to a boil, cover and remove from heat. Let stand for 5 minutes. Remove from saucepan and let cool.

In a medium bowl, mix together sugar, flour and salt. Stir in cooled raisin and juice mixture and mix well. Pour into prepared tart crust. Bake for 10 minutes. Reduce heat to 350° and continue baking for 25 to 30 minutes longer.

FRUIT MINCEMEAT TART

There is no suet or bits of beef in this mincemeat. Fresh and dried fruits, and nuts give this densely textured tart its name.

2 large Bosc or Anjou pears
2 large Granny Smith apples
1/3 cup raisins
2/3 cup chopped walnuts
3 tbs. rum

3 tbs. brown sugar
1/2 tsp. ground cloves
2 tbs. quick cooking tapioca
1 unbaked tart crust

Heat oven to 425°. Peel, quarter and core pears and apples. Chop into 1/2-inch pieces. Place in a large bowl. Add raisins, walnuts, rum, sugar, cloves and tapioca and stir to mix.

Pour into prepared tart crust and bake for 45 to 55 minutes. Remove from oven. Serve warm or at room temperature.

LINZER TART

An almond paste crust/base and raspberry jam make this classic tart perfect for special desserts.

¹/₄ cup butter
2 egg yolks
2 tbs. apple juice concentrate
2 tsp. vanilla extract
1 cup flour
¹/₂ tsp. baking powder
¹/₄ tsp. salt
1¹/₂ cups almonds, ground
10 oz. raspberry all-fruit jam or preserves

Heat oven to 350°. In a medium bowl, beat butter until light and fluffy. Blend in egg yolks, juice concentrate and vanilla.

In a small bowl, mix together flour, baking powder and salt. Stir in almonds. Add to butter mixture, mixing well. Spread 1½ cups of the batter evenly onto bottom of tart pan. Spread fruit evenly over batter, leaving 1-inch border around edge. Spoon remaining batter into pastry bag fitted with ½-inch plain or star tip. Pipe batter in lattice design over fruit spread. Chill in refrigerator for 30 minutes.

Place tart in oven and bake for 35 minutes, until crust is golden brown and fruit spread is bubbly. Cool completely on wire rack. Serve at room temperature.

PINEAPPLE TART

This tart is especially good when made with a macadamia-flavored Pastry Nut Crust, *page 4. Serve with a scoop of coconut ice cream for a Pina Colada dessert.*

½ cup granulated sugar
⅓ cup cornstarch
pineapple juice
1 can (8 oz.) crushed pineapple, drained, liquid reserved
4 egg yolks
1 tbs. butter
1 pre-baked tart crust

In a medium saucepan, combine sugar and cornstarch. Add enough pineapple juice to reserved pineapple liquid to make 1½ cups. Add to saucepan and stir to mix well. Bring to a boil over medium heat, stirring constantly. Remove from heat.

In a small bowl, beat egg yolks. Spoon a small amount of hot pineapple mixture into egg yolks and then return egg yolk mixture to saucepan, stirring constantly. Add butter and stir to melt. Return to stove and continue to cook over medium heat until mixture is thickened: do not boil. Stir in crushed pineapple. Pour into prepared tart crust and refrigerate until chilled.

LEMON CREAM TART

Creamy, tart, sweet, smooth — all describe this rich lemon tart. Try it in a macadamia-flavored Pastry Nut Crust, page 4, for a nice change of pace. Top with some fresh berries and whipped cream.

2 large lemons
3/4 cup granulated sugar
1/3 cup cornstarch
1 cup water
3 egg yolks
1 tbs. butter
1 cup sour cream
1 pre-baked tart crust

Squeeze juice from lemons and measure ⅓ cup juice. Discard any extra juice. Grate zest from lemons and add to juice. Set aside.

In a small saucepan, mix together sugar and cornstarch until blended. Add water, juice and zest. Cook over medium heat, stirring constantly, until mixture boils.

In a medium bowl, beat egg yolks until smooth. Whisk about ¼ cup of the hot syrup into egg yolks. Mix well. Whisk another ½ cup syrup into egg mixture, stirring constantly. Add remaining hot syrup to egg mixture and mix well. Pour mixture back into saucepan and return to medium heat. Cook, stirring constantly, until mixture is thick enough to heavily coat the back of a spoon.

Remove from heat and whisk in butter, stirring until melted. Let mixture cool at room temperature for 45 minutes. Whisk in sour cream and mix well. Pour into prepared tart crust and refrigerate until chilled, about 4 hours.

LEMON TART

Another classic tart, this is similar in taste and texture to a lemon meringue pie. This tart, however, has a firmer texture and a lot more lemon taste.

2 cups freshly squeezed lemon juice
1½ cups granulated sugar
6 eggs
6 egg yolks
2 tbs. grated lemon zest
¼ cup butter
1 pre-baked tart crust

In a medium stainless steel saucepan, mix lemon juice and sugar. Bring to a boil over high heat, reduce heat and simmer. Remove syrup from heat.

In a medium bowl, beat together eggs, egg yolks and lemon zest. Whisk about 1/2 cup of the hot syrup into egg mixture. Mix well. Whisk another 1/2 cup syrup into egg mixture, stirring constantly. Add remaining hot syrup to egg mixture and mix well.

Pour mixture back into saucepan and return to medium heat. Cook, stirring constantly, until mixture is thick enough to heavily coat the back of a spoon. Remove from heat and whisk in butter, a tablespoon at a time, until mixture is silky smooth. If needed, pour through a fine sieve into a bowl to remove any lumps.

Pour mixture into prepared crust and place a sheet of waxed paper or plastic wrap on top of custard. Refrigerate until firm, about 4 hours.

LIME TART

This is so refreshing! You can top this with fresh raspberries or sliced strawberries for a pretty summer dessert.

²/₃ cup all-purpose flour	2 egg yolks
1¼ cups granulated sugar	1 tbs. butter
¼ tsp. salt	1 cup freshly squeezed lime juice
1 cup water	1 pre-baked tart crust

In a medium saucepan, combine flour, sugar and salt. Add water and, using a wire whisk, stir until smooth. Cook over medium-low heat, stirring constantly, until mixture is thick and smooth.

In a small bowl, beat egg yolks. Spoon a small amount of hot mixture into egg yolks and then pour egg yolks back into saucepan, stirring constantly. Add butter and stir to melt. Return to the stove and cook over medium heat until mixture thickens: do not boil. Stir in lime juice. Pour mixture into prepared tart crust and refrigerate until chilled.

FROZEN MARGARITA TART

This has all the flavor of a margarita, with no alcohol. Serve this after a hearty Mexican meal for a light, refreshing dessert.

one 14 oz can sweetened condensed milk
$^1/_2$ cup freshly squeezed lime juice
grated zest of one lime
2 tbs. freshly squeezed orange juice
2 cups heavy whipping cream
1 pre-baked tart crust

Combine condensed milk, lime juice, lime zest and orange juice in a medium bowl. In another bowl, beat whipping cream to stiff peaks. Fold into lime mixture. Pour into prepared crust, and freeze for at least 2 hours.

BANANA CREAM TART

Don't think of slices of banana under vanilla pudding!! This tart is made of a rich banana and brown sugar custard, and then topped with fresh bananas and whipped cream. Every bite is loaded with banana flavor. It's important to use ripe bananas, but don't use black or very soft bananas.

$^1/_2$ cup brown sugar, packed
$^1/_3$ cup flour
$^1/_2$ tsp. salt
2 eggs
2 cups milk
3 large or 4 medium ripe bananas
1 pre-baked tart crust
whipped cream for topping, optional

In a medium saucepan, mix together brown sugar, flour and salt. In a small bowl, beat eggs and add them to sugar mixture. Add milk and mix well.

Place saucepan on top of a double boiler. Cook on high until mixture is very thick, stirring constantly with a wire whisk to prevent lumps. Do not boil. When mixture thickly coats the back of a spoon, remove from heat. Thinly slice 2 large or 3 medium bananas into mixture. Stir to mix well, ensuring that all bananas are coated in custard. (It's OK if bananas break up.)

Pour into prepared tart crust. Spray a sheet of plastic wrap with a nonstick cooking spray. Place wrap spray-side down over the top of the filling to prevent a skin from forming. Refrigerate until firm, about 3 to 4 hours. When ready to serve, remove plastic wrap. Slice remaining banana and arrange on top of tart. Top with dollops of whipped cream, if desired.

ORANGE CRANBERRY TART

This brightly colored tart is perfect for winter desserts, when you can get the best fresh oranges and cranberries.

Filling
1/3 cup granulated sugar
1/3 cup cornstarch
1 1/2 cups freshly squeezed orange juice
4 egg yolks

1 pre-baked tart crust

Topping
one pkg. (16 oz.) fresh cranberries
1 cup granulated sugar
1/4 cup cranberry or orange juice

In a medium saucepan, combine sugar and cornstarch. Add in orange juice. Stir to mix well. Place mixture over medium heat. Stirring constantly, bring mixture to a boil. Remove from heat.

In a small bowl, beat egg yolks. Spoon a small amount of the hot orange juice mixture into egg yolks. Then, pour egg yolk mixture into saucepan, stirring constantly. Return to the stove, and continue to cook on medium heat until mixture is thickened: do not boil. Pour mixture into prepared tart crust, and refrigerate until chilled.

While tart is cooling, prepare cranberry topping. Combine cranberries, sugar, and juice in a medium saucepan. Bring mixture to a boil and reduce heat to low. Cover and simmer for 30 minutes, or until berries have popped, and mixture has thickened. Cool in pan slightly, then spoon on top of orange base. Refrigerate until chilled.

ORANGE CREAM TART
WITH STRAWBERRIES

Tarts are a wonderful showcase for fruit pairs. This tart has an orange chiffon base, which you then top with halved strawberries. Not only is the fruit combination delicious, the presentation is beautiful.

1 baked tart crust
1 envelope unflavored gelatin
3/4 cup granulated sugar
3 egg yolks
1 tsp. grated orange peel
1 cup freshly squeezed orange juice
1 egg white
1/2 cup heavy cream
1 pint fresh strawberries

In a medium saucepan, combine unflavored gelatin with sugar until blended. In a small bowl, beat together egg yolks with orange peel and orange juice. Stir into gelatin mixture in saucepan.

Cook over medium-low heat, stirring constantly, until mixture is thickened and coats the back of a spoon. Remove from heat and refrigerate. Stir mixture occasionally until mixture cools, about 45 minutes.

In a large bowl, using an electric mixer, beat egg white until soft peaks form. Fold egg whites into gelatin mixture.

In the same bowl, add cream and beat until soft peaks form. Fold the whipped cream into gelatin mixture. Spoon mixture into prepared tart crust and level to top of crust. Clean and hull strawberries. Slice each berry in half from the top down. Arrange berries on top of orange mixture. Refrigerate until set, about 1 hour.

STRAWBERRY LEMON TART

Fans of strawberry lemonade will love this summer tart.

1 cup granulated sugar
3 tbs. cornstarch
¾ cup water
¼ cup freshly squeezed lemon
  juice

grated zest of 1 lemon
3 cups fresh strawberries (washed,
  hulled, and thickly sliced)
1 pre-baked tart crust

In a medium saucepan, stir together sugar and cornstarch. Add water and bring to a boil over medium-high heat. Reduce heat to medium and continue to cook until thick, about 8 to 10 minutes. Remove from heat and stir in lemon juice and zest. Taste and add additional lemon juice if desired.

Gently stir in strawberries and pour mixture into prepared tart crust. Refrigerate until firm, at least 3 hours.

FRESH PEACH TART

This tart uses fresh peaches under a cinnamon-flavored glaze. This should be made and served on the same day.

1 cup granulated sugar
2 tbs. cornstarch
¾ cup water
1 tsp. lemon juice
1 tsp. cinnamon

1 tsp. butter
3–4 large ripe peaches, peeled
1 pre-baked tart crust
whipped cream for topping

In a medium saucepan, combine sugar and cornstarch. Add water and lemon juice and stir until smooth. Cook over medium heat, stirring constantly, until very thick and clear. Remove from heat and stir in cinnamon and butter. Stir until well mixed and set aside. Cut peaches into ¼-inch-thick slices. Place on a paper towel and blot gently to absorb excess juice. Add to glaze mixture and gently stir to coat. Pour into prepared tart crust. Chill until firm. Serve with whipped cream, if desired.

APRICOT TART

Dried apricots flavor the creamy filling, with canned apricot halves decorating the top. I like this made with a macadamia-flavored Pastry Nut Crust, *page 4.*

12–16 canned apricot halves, drained*
8 dried apricot halves
1/3 cup granulated sugar
3 tbs. flour
2 egg yolks
2/3 cup half-and-half
1/2 cup heavy whipping cream
1 pre-baked tart crust
1/3 cup apricot preserves

* Set apricot halves onto a paper towel to absorb excess moisture. Replace paper towel as it becomes saturated.

Cut dried apricots into chunks. Place apricots and sugar into the bowl of a food processor workbowl or blender container. Pulse until apricots are chopped very fine. Add flour and pulse just until mixed.

In a medium saucepan, combine egg yolks with half-and-half. Mix well. Using a wire whisk, stir in apricot mixture. Stirring constantly, cook over medium heat until mixture is very thick. Remove from heat. Cover and refrigerate for 1 hour. Remove from refrigerator and whisk until smooth.

Whip heavy cream until stiff. Fold cream into apricot mixture. Spread filling over prepared crust. Arrange canned apricot halves over filling. Heat preserves in a small saucepan over medium heat. Strain preserves and discard any apricot pieces. Brush strained preserves over apricot halves. Refrigerate until well chilled, at least 4 hours.

BLUEBERRY TART

Lemon juice and zest help to brighten the flavor of the berries.

3 pints blueberries
¼ cup water
¾ cup sugar
2 tbs. quick cooking tapioca
¼ tsp. salt
1 tbs. grated lemon zest
1 tbs. freshly squeezed lemon juice
1 pre-baked tart crust

In a medium saucepan, combine berries and water. Cover and bring to a boil over medium-high heat.

Combine sugar, tapioca and salt together in a small bowl. Add sugar mixture to boiling berries and stir constantly to mix. Reduce heat to medium-low and continue to cook, stirring constantly, for about 5 minutes, until mixture is thickened. Remove from heat and stir in lemon zest and juice.

Pour berry mixture into prepared tart crust. Place a sheet of waxed paper or plastic wrap on top of tart and refrigerate until firm. For best flavor and texture, remove from refrigerator about 1 hour before serving.

CAPPUCCINO TART

Coffee liqueur and instant coffee give this mousse-like tart its flavor. You can also serve this in a chocolate wafer crust for a mocha flavor.

1 envelope unflavored gelatin
½ cup granulated sugar
3 egg yolks
½ cup milk
1 tbs. instant coffee
½ cup Kahlua or other coffee-flavored liqueur
1 cup heavy cream
1 pre-baked tart crust

In a medium saucepan, combine unflavored gelatin with sugar until blended. In a small bowl, beat together egg yolks and milk. Stir milk mixture into gelatin mixture in saucepan. Cook over medium-low heat, stirring constantly, until mixture is thickened and coats the back of a spoon. Remove from heat and add coffee liqueur and instant coffee. Stir until instant coffee has dissolved. Refrigerate for 20 minutes.

In a large bowl, beat heavy cream until soft peaks form. Fold whipped cream into gelatin mixture. Spoon mixture into prepared tart crust and level to top of crust. Refrigerate until set, about 1 hour.

RUM CREAM TART

Rum, cream, and chocolate make a very adult dessert. This is delicious in a Sweet Cookie Crust, *page 3.*

1 envelope unflavored gelatin	1 cup milk
½ cup light rum	½ cup heavy cream
4 egg yolks	1 pre-baked tart crust
¾ cup granulated sugar	1 cup grated chocolate

Soften gelatin in rum and set aside. In a medium saucepan, beat egg yolks and sugar together until light. Add milk and stir to mix. Place saucepan on top of a double boiler and cook until thick, about 10 minutes. Remove from heat and stir in gelatin mixture, stirring until gelatin has completely dissolved and mixture is smooth. Let cool.

Meanwhile, beat cream until stiff. Fold into cooled custard mixture and turn into prepared tart crust. Sprinkle chocolate over custard. Refrigerate until firm, about 4 hours.

CHOCOLATE CHIP CHEESECAKE TART

This is a serious chocolate tart — small slices should be served. It has the taste of chocolate cheesecake, but is very easy to prepare. It is also a no-bake tart, so it is good to make with your kids.

2 pkg. (8 oz. pkg.) cream cheese,
   at room temperature
1 cup granulated sugar
$\frac{1}{3}$ cup cocoa powder
2 tbs. heavy cream

1 tbs. vanilla extract
1 cup mini chocolate chips
1 pre-baked *Sweet Cookie Crust,*
   page 3
whipped cream for topping

Combine cream cheese, sugar and cocoa powder in a large bowl. Using an electric mixer, beat until well mixed and smooth. Add cream, vanilla and chocolate chips and mix well. Spoon into prepared crust and refrigerate until firm, about 4 hours. Serve with lots of whipped cream.

CHOCOLATE PEANUT BUTTER TART

This is one for the kids–or you can make it and pretend you have kids. To make a fun presentation, cut peanut butter cups in half and arrange around the edge of your tart.

2 cups half-and-half
4 egg yolks
⅓ cup unsweetened cocoa powder
1¼ cups granulated sugar
⅓ cup cornstarch
½ cup "natural-style" peanut butter
1 pre-baked tart crust

In a medium saucepan, combine half-and-half and eggs. Beat until well mixed.

In a small bowl, mix together cocoa powder, sugar and cornstarch. Add to half-and-half mixture. Place saucepan in the top half of a double boiler and cook until mixture is very thick, and heavily coats the back of a metal spoon. Do not allow mixture to boil.

Remove from heat and stir in peanut butter. Pour mixture into prepared tart crust. Refrigerate for at least 4 hours.

WHITE CHOCOLATE RASPBERRY TART

White chocolate makes this sound exotic, but it just adds a vanilla creaminess to the custard base.

3 egg yolks	1 tbs. butter
1/2 cup granulated sugar	1/2 cup white chocolate chips
2 tbs. cornstarch	1/2 cup heavy cream
1 cup milk	2 cups fresh raspberries
1 tsp. vanilla extract	1 pre-baked tart crust

In a small bowl, mix together egg yolks and sugar until light. Whisk in cornstarch, beating until smooth. Set aside.

In a medium saucepan, bring milk and vanilla to a boil over medium-high heat. Whisk a small amount of the hot milk mixture into egg yolks and beat until smooth. Add egg yolks back to milk mixture and whisk until smooth. Continue to cook over medium-high heat, stirring constantly, until mixture returns to a boil. Cook for 1 to 2 minutes, until very thick. Remove from heat and stir in butter and chocolate chips, stirring until both are completely melted and well mixed into milk mixture. If needed, strain custard. Pour custard into a bowl and place a sheet of plastic wrap over the top to prevent a skin from forming. Refrigerate until cold.

Remove custard from refrigerator and whisk until smooth. Whip cream until stiff peaks form. Fold whipped cream and 1½ cups of the raspberries into cold custard. Spoon into prepared tart crust. Place remaining ½ cup of berries on top of custard. Return to refrigerator until firm, about 2 to 4 hours.

DARK CHOCOLATE AND ORANGE TART

For best flavor and texture, use high quality preserves when making this tart.

2 cups heavy cream
8 oz. bittersweet chocolate

¾ cup orange marmalade or
    preserves, divided
1 pre-baked tart crust

In a medium saucepan, bring cream to a boil over medium-high heat. Remove from heat, add chocolate and stir until melted. Add ½ cup of the marmalade and stir to mix. Pour through a fine sieve and discard any remaining orange bits. Refrigerate until chilled, about 45 minutes.

Spread remaining ¼ cup marmalade on bottom of prepared tart crust. Using an electric mixer, beat chocolate cream until smooth. Pour into crust. Smooth top of filling. Refrigerate for at least 4 hours before serving.

RASPBERRY CREAM TART

This light tart has a filling similar to a mousse. This makes a perfect dessert when having a heavy or rich meal.

1 tbs. unflavored gelatin	3/4 cup powdered sugar
2 tbs. water	1 pre-baked tart crust
1 cup crushed raspberries	1 cup fresh raspberries
1 cup heavy cream	

In a medium bowl, dissolve gelatin in water for 5 minutes. Add crushed berries and stir to mix.

In a large bowl, whip cream until very stiff. Whip in sugar, mixing well. Fold crushed berry mixture into cream and then pour into prepared tart crust. Smooth top and place fresh berries on top. Refrigerate until firm, about 4 hours.

FRESH FRUIT TART

This is a simple vanilla cream base, topped with your favorite fresh fruits. All berries work well, as do slices of ripe peach, nectarine, plum or kiwi fruit. Use one fruit or a mixture. Use your imagination in topping the sweet cream and you'll have a beautiful, custom-made dessert.

1 egg
4 egg yolks
$\frac{1}{2}$ cup granulated sugar
$\frac{1}{4}$ cup flour
2 cups half-and-half
2 tsp. vanilla extract
1 pre-baked tart crust
2–3 cups fresh fruit (raspberries, blackberries, strawberries, kiwi, peaches or other)

In a medium saucepan, beat together egg and egg yolks until light. In a small bowl, mix together sugar and flour. Add to eggs and mix well. Using a wire whisk, beat in half-and-half until mixture is smooth.

Place saucepan in the top half of a double boiler and cook over high heat, stirring constantly. Don't let mixture boil, but cook until very thick. Remove from heat and stir in vanilla.

Pour into prepared tart crust. Cover with a sheet of waxed paper or plastic wrap and refrigerate until firm, about 4 hours. Just before serving, top with pieces of fruit, peeled and sliced as appropriate. Arrange fruit in an attractive pattern.

FRUIT AND CHEESE TART

This tart is fast and easy to prepare, so you can have a beautiful dessert in a few minutes. Freshly pitted and halved Bing cherries make a wonderful pairing with the cheese, but use any fresh fruit you enjoy.

8 oz. cream cheese
1 tbs. grated lemon zest
½ cup powdered sugar
1 pre-baked tart crust

2 cups fresh fruit of choice
¼ cup granulated sugar
2 tbs. freshly squeezed lemon
   juice

In a medium bowl, using an electric mixer, beat together cream cheese, lemon zest and powdered sugar until light and fluffy. Spread cheese mixture over prepared tart crust, covering bottom and sides with an equal layer.

Clean, peel and slice fruit if necessary. Gently toss fruit with sugar and lemon juice, tossing only enough to dissolve sugar. Pour fruit mixture into crust. Refrigerate and serve within 2 hours.

COCONUT PINEAPPLE TART

This is especially good in a Sweet Cookie Crust, *page 3.*

1 cup crushed pineapple,
  squeezed dry*
16 oz. cream cheese
$1/2$ cup canned cream of coconut

$1/3$ cup granulated sugar
1 cup sweetened flaked coconut
1 pre-baked tart crust

   * Let pineapple drain in a sieve for 30 minutes; then, using a spoon or spatula, press pineapple down to remove additional liquid. Finish by squeezing pineapple with your hands to remove all remaining liquid.

   Using an electric mixer, beat cream cheese until smooth. Mix in cream of coconut and sugar until well blended. Stir in coconut and pineapple. Spoon into prepared crust.

   Refrigerate until filling is firm, at least 3 hours.

BERRY TIRAMISU TART

This was created for someone who loves the Italian dessert Tiramisu, but wished there was no coffee flavoring.

1/4 cup cornstarch
1/4 cup granulated sugar
1 1/2 cups heavy cream
2 egg yolks
8 oz. mascarpone cheese, at room temperature
2 tbs. rum
2 tsp. vanilla extract
1 pre-baked tart crust
1 cup blackberries
1/3 cup blackberry jam
3 tbs. sugar

In a medium saucepan, combine cornstarch and sugar. Mix in cream. Cook over medium heat, stirring constantly, until thickened but not boiling.

In a small bowl, beat egg yolks until smooth. Pour $1/4$ cup of the hot cream mixture into beaten eggs, stirring well to mix. Add eggs back to saucepan, stirring constantly. Continue to cook over medium heat, stirring constantly, until mixture is very thick, about 2 minutes. Take care not to boil. Remove from heat and stir in mascarpone cheese, rum and vanilla. Mix well and pour into prepared crust. Refrigerate until firm, about 4 hours.

Combine berries, jam and sugar in a small saucepan. Heat over medium-low heat, stirring frequently, until berries burst and sugar has dissolved. Remove from heat and refrigerate until chilled.

To serve, cut the chilled tart into wedges and top with berry sauce.

INDEX